I0620453

Beyond the Brink: The Woman Who Refused to Quit

By

Catherine L Bennett

Copyright © 2025 Catherine L Bennett

Prologue

I was born on January 17th, 1956, in *Wichita, Kansas*. I am the oldest of three children and the firstborn of Walter *Edward Davidson* and *Roberta Ann Gleason*.

I got married in December 1973 and graduated high school in May 1974. I started having children in 1975, having three children and one miscarriage in 1976. I had a second daughter in 1978 and a son in 1982. I was divorced in 1998 and started college in 1999.

I graduated in 2003 with a Bachelor of Science in hospitality in restaurant management. I remarried in 2008 and became a widower in 2023. I was a member of the *Lions Club Missionette* program, a Girl Scout leader, and also one in Boy Scouts. I took several training courses in each program and loved teaching others. I hope to pass on words of wisdom from things I have learned about myself, which can only be learned through the books of hard knocks.

If you do not believe in a higher being, please listen anyway. I believe I would not be here if not for the higher being. I believe that God was the purpose for me here on earth more than in heaven. I also believe that this book is one that was meant to be. It is a series of short stories about me recounting the physical abuse I endured as a child and how it persisted in various forms even in adulthood.

I will tell stories of emotional abuse from a stepmother and a first and second husband while also being bullied and teased by others in my early teens and early adulthood, causing insecurity and mistrust, shyness, and fear throughout most of my life.

Some stories will be told in ways that few have ever heard. While some stories are so terrible in their misdeeds that I would never wish them on anyone, I'm standing strong because of these stories.

Acknowledgment

I would like to fully acknowledge my dear friend, Chaplain Joe Chapman, who has been a great listener, offering valuable spiritual guidance whenever needed. Brother Joe has been listening to me weekly for over three years now.

Chaplain Joe is with the spiritual care team at *Mercy Hospital* in *Saint Louis, Missouri*. Brother Joe has helped me more than any other counselor or therapist during the last several years over the spelling of ups and downs that I have been going through.

He was the one who diagnosed me with the latest diagnosis of post-ICU syndrome. I didn't even know there was such a diagnosis. I thought I was having symptoms of post-traumatic stress or PSTD from my childhood, but I learned that this was a new type of post-traumatic disorder brought on by trauma in the ICU after my near-death car wreck 5 years ago.

I spent 7 months in either the ICU, a rehab hospital, or a rehab nursing home for physical therapy. I am still learning to walk and may not walk more than I am now. Brother Joe has helped me to cope with the real reality of how long this may take and helped me deal with some of the issues that have come to light as I began to write this book. Some of the things in this book would never have been told if not for the result of his listening. Brother Joe helped me to see the good in sharing so it can help others and that is exactly what I'm doing.

I am also grateful to Mr. Kevin Jones from Ebook Writing Experts in assisting me to write and published this book and let my dream come true to write this book.

Dedication

I would like to dedicate this book to my family, especially my children. As I learn more about myself, I learn how I messed up raising them. I thought I was doing my best and learned I could have done more. May this book open the eyes of others to the fact that no one is perfect and we can all learn from our mistakes.

May my children forgive me if I didn't learn fast enough. May this book help those I haven't taught so that they figure it out independently. Use this book as self-help for the ways we need to follow a higher being. I believe all gods lead to the one almighty god, God our Father. Catholics, Baptists, Methodists, Protestants, Jews, and Buddhas all have their '*God*' that they pray to, but their Gods are just one God.

And finally, I'd like to dedicate this to:

Emmanuel-Jesus Christ (*"Behold, a virgin shall be with child, and shall bring forth a son, and they shall call his name Emmanuel, which being interpreted is, God with us."* **Matthew1:23**)

Table of Contents

About the Author

My name is Catherine Bennett. I am filled with family, service, and a deep love for the world around me.

I am not just a mother but also a grandmother and even a great-grandmother, a role that brings me nothing but immense joy.

I also have had the privilege of helping raise my step-granddaughter and step-grandson, welcoming them as part of my heart and home.

A few things define me, and one of them is education, which has always been a cornerstone of my journey, shaping how I see the world and contribute to it.

For over thirty years, I have dedicated myself to the Boy Scouts, not just as an adult leader but as a mentor, a guide, and a believer in the power of teaching. I am, at my core, an educator. I find purpose in helping others learn and grow, whether through scouting, my personal pursuits, or the many activities that have defined my path.

I believe in family, kindness, the power of forgiveness, and the importance of helping others find their way. Life, to me, is an adventure best approached with an open heart and an easygoing spirit.

If you know me, you will also know that I find relief and inspiration in nature. There's always more to this world. The beauty of the world reminds me to cherish each and every moment, embrace the simple joys, and keep moving forward with gratitude.

This represents who I am and serves as the blueprint for my life.

Chapter 1: The Day Everything Changed

It is unknown how such a simple question can still open a floodgate of things that have been kept hidden and locked away for a very long time. My story begins with sitting around a camp picnic table during an Adult Boy Scout training event called *Woodbadge*. The instructor said, *"During the third grade, what were your most memorable thoughts?"* Silence descended around the picnic table as everybody joined in to describe the games they played at the playgrounds, the admired teachers, and numerous childhood friends. But for me, that question was not a cue to tell a number of funny stories I have encountered in my life. It was the key to a door I had closed solidly for a past I never wanted to confront or share aloud with others. I was ashamed of my past. I wanted to keep it private.

Recalling how I felt when I was around other students in the camp, as they sat around the camp table taking the training, I was surprised at how this simple question left me in a spin. My heart raced, and all sorts of feelings of panic flooded my heart. The moments of my life, which were already painful, were again described in such a way that it appeared to me as if I were again going through all those episodes of my life. Suddenly, the tears welled up in my eyes, and the worst feeling possible rose in me: the desire to flee from the past because the overwhelming flow of emotion was unbearable. I was numb and almost speechless, thinking about something that I had tried so hard to avoid in the past. I left that weekend with thoughts of never returning, avoiding sharing my feelings. But I would have to confront my story the next weekend or quit.

I did go back, and with the addition of my anxiety medication and a lot of guts, I proceeded to the end. As it materialized, it proved to be one of the greatest decisions I had taken. The group was an important support and a key to comprehension. The friendships that were created were lifelong, and it was within those confines of support that I started to understand the cause of my problems.

In fact, the third grade was the turning point in my life. Until that time, I suppose my life was rather mundane, or at least as mundane as a life could be. Our two-story house was built right next to the fish hatchery in *Neosho*, Missouri. It was a poorly built old house, with drafts entering through the broken windows when night became frosty. Upstairs, we had our small partitioned space where my siblings and I slept. There were only two rooms: one for two beds where we slept and the other for toys. It wasn't much, but it was our world; *it was our private, personal space, and it was very important to us.*

The night was particularly cold and rainy. My little brother was in second grade at that time, and he woke up crying. The boy was wet from an accident on his bed, and he was shivering. As soon as I could, I got him into dry clothing and put him to bed with my sister, who was only five years old. She was fast asleep even though the night was cold. As I moved back to lay down a beep sound of a car door locking was audible to my ears. I peeked from the window and watched our mother's car moving slowly towards town. I didn't quite know where she was going and at that age, it really did not occur to me to stop her. I returned to the bed with my siblings.

That was what had become known as the night that changed everything in my life. It was nothing more than a normal occurrence back then; a mother went to run an errand when the children slept. I never thought that it would turn into a nightmare. We were unaware that our father would turn this moment against our mother in the legal proceedings that would change our lives. The next weekend, three children would tell what we saw through our young eyes and with innocent hearts what we thought we knew: that she had left during the night. We failed to understand the implication of what I said or how it would be used to paint a picture of an unfit mother by twisting our words to fill their purpose.

That information our father took to a judicial authorities' seat, where he used it to demonstrate that she was an irresponsible and unfit mother. It was only later that we found out that this was not nearly as big of a scandal as we had been told. Our mother had only gone out to buy milk for the next morning's breakfast. She was not a worthless piece of trash who left us alone to go drink herself to death at a bar, as our father claimed. But by then, it was too late. The judge had favored Dad in the custody case, and all of a sudden, we were stripped of the only woman who loved us. I don't know if my siblings ever knew the truth.

This event drove all of the kids apart. My mother was not the most beautiful woman, the most intelligent, the most responsible, but she loved us, and her love is irreplaceable. Instead, in her place came a terrible woman who could hardly be called a stepmother. At first, she was so sweet, but then the real person came out. The woman was very stern in her behavior and would rather someone administer discipline to my siblings, such as myself. Because I fought back, my stepmother tied me to the bed, hitting me where the belt or flyswatter hit, on the back, the arm, the head, and usually hard enough to leave a mark.

Beyond the Brink: The Woman Who Refused to Quit

Sometimes, she would hit me with a dirty potato masher for silly mistakes, like when the dishwasher wouldn't do its job, and I used to be a scapegoat for things I did not do to avoid being beaten. The most offensive was that she wanted us to call her 'Mom' as if the word could compensate for all that was taken away from us. It was forbidden to call her stepmom. She wanted no one to think about her in any wicked manner.

I had to get out of the habit of arguing or saying anything wrong and try to behave as positively as possible. It was up to me to shield my other siblings from her rage as much as I could. I was the one who stood in front and took as many hits as necessary to protect my siblings.

The years went by, and I never really got over it; that night haunts me to this date. When I was about to graduate high school, my mother was driving to the school unannounced. I hadn't seen her in more than ten years, yet she stopped and called me at school, hoping to make amends. But with my stepmother going to be at the graduation, I couldn't afford to take that chance. My mother might try to see my siblings. Even though I was angry, I did not want a scene that would disrupt the balance achieved with my dad and stepmother. Despite this, it was painful, and I had to make my mother go back home. I still remember her voice over the phone when I told her I would not have her come down. There was every hue of emotion, from disappointment and sadness to understanding. She understood why I had to do it, but still, it was not easy. I could tell she was crying. I knew she could get arrested if she tried to see my siblings before they were 18

I bore the consequence of that decision for many years. I didn't fully comprehend this for a number of years later in my life and saw how much it impacted me. My siblings were never told. In more ways than one, post-conflict avoidance had become the norm, and I didn't even know what I wanted. I was never taught how to defend myself, mostly because my childhood responsibility was to defend my siblings. It was in the third grade that my life changed, making this discovery that the world is not always nice and can be really vicious, that the people, whom you trusted, can betray you, and that sometimes, in order to defend yourself, you have to smile, pretending everything is fine, but in reality, it was not. I learned to be strong, but at the same time, it stripped me of my childhood way too early.

I was to learn later in life that I had been stripped of so much more than just my childhood. Still today, I find new scars in my soul that the PTSD has caused because of my past.

Chapter 2: A Life in Pieces

Before the beginning of my senior year in high school, I was very disoriented. From an early age, I had witnessed more suffering than most children should in a lifetime. However, I continued to look to the future as a slightly better time in my life was still possible. I would try to put two rapes and an attempted murder behind me. Summer vacation was another turning point in my life.

My loneliness began to decrease. I started to interact with people and be more social of some sort. Nevertheless, because of what I have experienced before, I was stimulated by a strong desire to be loved and accepted. This made me powerless and easy prey for other people who never cared or respected me. I had two brief experiences of affection that same year that made me feel used and violated. It was hard trying to figure out why misfortune befalls me, and I started to assume that I was to blame for all the hardships.

On the other hand, having to deal with the realities for years, much earlier than I would usually have to, had built a strength within me that would prove helpful. I was committed to avoiding being harmed or harming the ones I loved. Once, one of my ex-boyfriends threatened me with violence after a breakup; one of my classmates protected me and defended me, fighting the aggressor.

Even though he was expelled for it, which I'll never forget, it was an act of courage he had done for me. It also gave me hope that there is still such a thing as being conscious and courteous to fellow human beings. He threatened to take my life and waited outside the theatre until he saw my father, not knowing I had called him.

Before leaving high school, I thought college would allow me to change my life. But life had other plans. During the beginning half of my senior year, I met a decent man, Jim, during a double-blind date with a girlfriend and her fiancé. Jim was polite and made me feel valued. The things that connected us for the entire duration of our marriage were our hobbies involving nature and involvement in our society. Since I have had my fair share of being let down by those around me, I slowly learned to trust again. On 29th December 1973, during Christmas vacation, we joined our faith in holy matrimony in a small ceremony with only my parents present. For the first time, I can escape tragedy to hope and dream that my life might settle down and even become happier as an oilfield wife. I would graduate from high school as a married woman.

We were happy in the early years of our marriage, and Jim's love and encouragement healed some broken facets in me. That is why Jim spent long hours at work, and I was happy to have a stable home to take care of our children. There was a lot of pressure and much responsibility, but the fun activities, as well as camping, scouting, and community services, gave purpose to me. That independence and adventure were still attractions, but now my concerns were to take care of our children to give them a comfortable home and loving family, which I never had.

Since 1989, I have devoted more than 30 years of volunteer service to the Boy Scouts. As an adult I would take the kids to the Girl Scouts meetings, along with ballet lessons and church groups that kept us busy in courage, resilience, and unselfishness. Volunteering activities turned into a goal for me as well as helping our family bond. However, as years went by, so did the responsibilities at Jim's workplace and the different interests that led to our separation.

He was gone longer, and I felt our marriage slipping away even while I tried to make it work. It seemed that the harder I tried, the worse our marriage got. Our interests and desire to be closer to each other grew farther apart. Little did I know that Jim had been cheating on me for over 6 years.

Jim and I had been together for 25 years; in 1998, he asked for a divorce, which destroyed the hope I had built for the future. I was crushed not only to have lost my partner but the picture of a stable family that I had fought for many years. All my family and friends supported Jim as I tried to cope with extremely painful feelings of loss, frustration, and fear for my future all by myself.

While mourning for 3 months, I also went through intense self-analysis. I had no control over the divorce, but I did have control over what came next for me. Lying in the recliner, dressed in a blanket and a robe, was not the life to lead. I had to get up and move forward for my children and for myself. I had now learned to get up and start all over again, and I was determined to do just that. I wanted a better life for my kids and needed to be strong enough to show them how they deserved a better life.

Seeing how many people started working after a divorce and getting an education only after some time, I thought it would be a good time for me to start on the path of achieving my childhood dream of getting an education. I enrolled for college at the age of 42 and attended classes while working part-time and taking care of my children all at the same time. However, the journey was tough through my volunteering activities to understand how one single-minded person can make a difference by not wanting my children to think that they were too old to go to college. Thus, I made up my mind, that with scholarships and patience, my kids saw me accomplish a bachelor's in hospitality, majoring in restaurant management.

I passed college in 2003 and earned a full-time job that came through the internship. The year before graduation Jim passed from his health problems in early 2002 and never saw me accomplish this dream. His absence was another gap in my fragile heart. I never knew that I needed him so much. But the empathy and the strength I had gained allowed me to overcome my loss.

All the broken parts of my childhood seemed irreparable, but I was slowly putting my life back together with perseverance. My experiences had established me a well of compassion, which I was privileged to draw from. I was willing to bring all lessons and mentalities gathered through the journey to assist people in their difficult moments. My new chapter was just starting. I was learning to stand on my own, even if it was with God alone. I was at peace knowing that.

Chapter 3: The First Steps: The New Perspective of Strength

I never realized how much I needed to take control of my life and find strength when I was at my lowest. My four years of college had been challenging at most. On the positive side, I've had the opportunity to make friends and gain a new perspective on the world, but also learned the challenges that life would bring.

During those years, I learned a lot and began to see myself in a new light. Realizing I was going to be on my own; I had no support. But slowly, I started to regain my strength as I stopped relying on my ex-husband. I did continue to lean on my kids for support. Despite this, my self-esteem and overall sense of self-worth were still quite low.

I began searching for new volunteer opportunities to keep myself occupied. I participated in girl scouting activities with girls and boy scouting with my son. I also enjoyed teaching at various adult scout events. I discovered that I love teaching, something I hadn't realized before. I started looking forward to teaching others what I know. I love researching new topics and sharing them, especially the topics that have to do with nature and teaching others.

By then, I had started seeing a counselor helping me address the challenges I was facing. The counselor guided me toward becoming the adult I wanted to be. I also got involved in many outdoor activities, monitored my weight, and learned to appreciate myself more. Watching what I ate made me feel good, which, in turn, boosted my self-esteem. I decided to start over with my Bible and attend church more often. I began to get real close to God, putting my whole faith in him.

It was 1996 when I started to look for God more often and rely on him for guidance. I discovered that God doesn't put more on you than you can handle. I also tried online dating, but that wasn't working out well. It had been 25 years, and I had forgotten what it was like to date by then. I was beginning to lose interest in dating, as I thought most men weren't interested in me anymore.

They seemed to want one thing only. It was at this time that I started to lose interest even in sex. It seemed like a burden. I realized that my search for fulfillment wasn't worth it without God. I started asking God if He had someone different in mind for me. I wanted Him to bring that somebody into my life because I was way too drained of searching around. After 25 years of being married, I had forgotten how to date, and by then I had given up on myself.

I wanted to be on the right path. I asked God to help me stay on the right side and let Him guide me wherever I go. I begin entirely to incline towards faith. I had taken the initiative to participate in summer camp, marking my first experience with it. On the very first day of that summer, I was driving to the camp with my son, who would work there alongside me. As I rounded a curve, the car began to fishtail, and before I knew it, the rear end of the car was passing by me.

I hit the brakes a little too hard and rolled the car, ending upside down in the middle of the road. I was hanging from my seatbelt and could hear the wheels still rolling, which scared me to no end. My son had somehow been thrown out of the car, and he was standing outside, telling me that I needed to get out. I laughed at him and said, *"Well, that's good, but the windows are all squished up, and what's not squashed up is filled with sand."*

The impact had completely smashed the car's hood. Bubba helped me crawl through the side window, and once we got out, we realized we were blocking the traffic. We had to direct vehicles around the car and send someone for help. Back in 1996, there were no cell phones like there are today, so we had to find someone to call for assistance, as the phones up in the mountains didn't work. Only a few cars had box phones in them.

My son and I stood opposite corners, directing traffic around the corner until the sheriff arrived. That was the first incident that summer for me, occurring at 10 a.m. on the first Sunday. The following Sunday, at the same time, I was cooking breakfast for the camp staff and preparing for the campers to arrive at noon.

I picked up the lid of a large electric griddle designed to cook for several hundred people. The cord got in the way when I attempted to close it. The radio cord we had on the shelf above it crossed out of nowhere, sending sparks flying all over the kitchen and frightening everyone there. They teased me for the rest of the day that I was just trying to electrify myself.

Things got odder with time. The very next Sunday, everyone was getting ready to head into town to buy groceries and do their laundry, just like they always did. Suddenly, out of nowhere, lightning struck just before a thunderstorm rolled in, and we found ourselves in the health lodge. The lightning traveled down the chimney, through the rebar, and up to the floor, ultimately hitting the metal desk and leaving through the computer's keyboard.

The camp director occupied the room next to ours, and we eventually ended up sending him to the hospital. We were close enough to the lightning strike that a bruise on my arm, which I had received in the recent car accident, was highlighted by the beautiful shades of purple and green in its healing stage. Nevertheless, I noticed the bruise had disappeared entirely the next day. It was visible that morning and gone when I woke up the next day.

When we spoke with the health nurse who was present at the scene and asked how the bruise could disappear, he explained that we had absorbed electrons from the lightning, which caused the blood vessels in the bruise to evaporate. This eliminated the bruise completely. To me, that was shocking, as I was too close.

That was the day I realized how God had been looking out for me all this time. I experienced three incidents where I could have been hurt, but I emerged unscathed. This only boosted my spirits, reminding me that God was watching over me and caring for me in many ways. I felt safe and secure for a brief moment, intense emotions I hadn't experienced in quite some time.

Things were starting to improve. However, when I got home, I found that whenever I tried to read, it only gets hard for me to comprehend everything that I read. I understood the content, but I struggled to read it properly. I needed to read it over and over to grasp the material fully. This was how I approached reading my Bible, as comprehension was impossible.

I was friends with my Sunday school teacher who recognized that studying could be challenging for me, so we struck a deal. She agreed to call me weekly to inform me of the Bible verses we would study. This way, I could prepare and follow along during the lesson the following Sunday. We maintained this routine for about six weeks: she would call, and I would read and study the verses to ensure I could answer her questions in class.

Then again, the Bible verses she shared with me turned out to be answers to prayers I had been asking all week, things for which I needed guidance but hadn't known what the answers were.

One night, while watching TV of all movies, it was GI Jane—I felt a wave of fear come over me. At that moment, I received a vision and a thought from God: if she could make it through the challenges in that movie, I could surely make it through life as well. This realization brought me hope for the next day.

The movie gave me a lasting sense of hope, which I have deeply appreciated ever since. It made me realize that God can reach us regardless of our circumstances and He is always by our side. Also, it taught me that God can use everyday events and material things to guide and inspire us. It doesn't always have to come through the Bible; it can be found in anything here on Earth.

This event has taught me to use my life as evidence. I have reflected on various experiences, including my time as a scout and a major moment involving a lightning strike, to show how God has worked wonders in my life. I believe that He will always be with me in everything I do, even when I face challenges and difficulties.

I was confident that dating experiences had not been working for me, but I knew that God had answers. So, I decided to go to Mount Magazine, the highest place in my area, to pray all day. I believed that if anyone could answer me, it would be God. By this point, I felt assured that He was listening to me the whole time. The higher to Heaven, the better the chances of getting an answer.

Right after that trip, I was convinced I needed to go home and delete all my online dating accounts. I didn't want anything to do with it anymore; I wanted to wait for my perfect match. With the reassurance that it was in God's hands, I deleted everything from my computer. As I removed names and profiles, a little pop-up message appeared on my screen: "*I've never done this before. But something told me to give online dating a chance.*"

Something compelled me to delete it, but I couldn't. I almost deleted the pop-up at that moment, but when he mentioned that he had never done anything like this before, it made me pause and reconsider. Maybe I shouldn't delete his profile just *yet.* I continued with everyone else's profile related to dating *but not his.* I kept thinking, *I did ask God to put my match in front of me.*

I deleted several profiles but kept returning to one because it caught my attention. I thought I should check out his profile to see his appearance. Perhaps he was good-looking. When I visited his page, I saw that he was in a scout uniform.

This was something I had specifically requested in a prayer. I thought it would be nice if God had someone in mind for me who was involved in scouting, as it would give us something in common. My previous husband was never involved in scouting and didn't support my participation in those activities.

I thought a guy in a scout uniform was looking at my profile. That gave me a bit of hope. I decided I shouldn't delete him. However, I remembered that my son was paying for the internet, and I was about to lose my connection. My son had just lost his job.

I wanted to hear from him but I needed to let him know that I wouldn't have internet access next week so that I could maintain contact with him. I told him, *"I'll talk to you, but you'll need to call me since I'll be losing my internet connection."* I gave him my phone number, even though I probably shouldn't have, but I did it anyway.

After finishing my work, I turned off my computer and went to bed. Fifteen minutes later, the phone rang; it was *Bruce*. He called to let me know that he would be attending a summer camp and would be away all summer. He wanted to ask if he could take me out for Chinese food when he returned. I immediately told him *yes*.

Later that summer, his dad had a heart attack, which got him to come home early. After making sure that his mom was settled and doing fine, he checked on his dad in the hospital. Once satisfied that everything was fine, he came to get me, and we went out for Chinese food. From that point on, we began to see each other regularly. We dated for 3 years before he asked me to marry him.

Chapter 4: Angels Among Us

As my faith and love for God grew, I began to experience many good things in my life, and Bruce was certainly one of those blessings. He was like an *angel* to me, and I also felt like his angel. He treated me like a queen, as if I were someone to cherish and honor, placing me on a pedestal.

He treated me as though I were something special, delicate, and easy to break, someone who needed constant care. He would do anything for me, and he felt almost too *real*. He even cooked for me, cleaned, took me wherever we went, and taught me how to do scouts with him.

There was a time when the bank foreclosed on my house; he promised to take care of me and ensure I wouldn't starve. He had two bedrooms and a bathroom on the far end of his house. We could share the kitchen and living room; *his mom and dad lived in the apartment at the back of the house.* Bruce had built that apartment for his parents.

I knew I could be asked to leave at any moment, but I decided to use the rooms Bruce offered me and my grandson. However, I was concerned about the implications of a single woman living with a single man without being married, even with chaperones present. This situation made me feel insecure, so I told him I needed time to think it over.

After I went to bed that night, I prayed, asking for guidance. *"Lord, I need to know what to do."* In response, He gave me a vision. I imagined a triangle in the air, with me standing at the top point. If I stepped out onto the triangle's left side, everyone would be watching me. However, I would slide all the way to the bottom and ultimately fail because I hadn't put my trust in the Lord.

If you step out on the right side of that triangle, you will find yourself in front of God's presence—full of grace and assurance that everything will be okay, and nothing can hold you back. He will protect you with His divine wisdom. As you take that step, you will feel as if you're standing in midair, and you won't fail or fall. Others will see that you are walking alongside God, and you will have the confidence that it doesn't matter what anyone else thinks.

What other people see might be wrong. God knows what's going on, and he knows the truth. The other people might not know the truth, but it's what God thinks and truly knows. This is what is known as standing on blind faith.

The next day, I told Bruce I would move in, so we lived together for three years after moving in with him. During that time, my brother stopped speaking to me because he viewed me as a sinful woman. That all ended on a good note. Right after those three years, we got married and had a happy marriage lasting for fifteen years.

It was a marriage of angels. We thought and acted alike, completely mirroring each other. The day I moved in with him, his father died, and I thought, *"This can't be true."* Something feels off. I moved in with a man, and on that very day, his father passed away.

His incredibly kind mother took me aside and shared that he had been suffering from colon cancer. She explained that when I moved in, it brought Bruce's dad a sense of peace. He no longer worried about who would take care of her and Bruce after he was gone.

She said to me, *"When you moved in, he felt reassured that someone would care for Bruce and me, especially since he saw how happy we were during Christmas."* I was overwhelmed to hear that, as we had the best Christmas he had ever experienced, and it brought him so much joy. He was confident that he was leaving us in good hands, and he passed away with a smile on his face, expressing that he was finally at peace.

She made my day. She was my angel, and I was her angel, sent to find peace through each other. We can all be angels, as they walk among us daily without our knowledge. We don't always know who the real angels are.

I lost my place as well and had no home of my own. We all have our own beliefs and attend church together, sharing our problems. Something that Bruce and I discovered is that he's Catholic while I'm Assembly of God, which are opposite in terms of beliefs. He believes in praying through Mary, trusting she will intercede for his sins and help him.

I believe in raising my hand, talking in tongues, and praising God. And I think that God's in my heart, and I can speak to him at any time of the day I want, that I have that direct line that I can talk to him. And I know that he talks to me all the time.

He always reminds me when I'm not supposed to be doing something or need to be careful. He was there the day I had my car accident about five years ago, the night I should have died. In truth, I probably did die. I drove 30 miles on winding roads and blacked out during the drive. I don't remember anything from that time, but I am alive and well here.

I am learning to walk again after suffering numerous broken bones, it's unbelievable. But I am here, I am alive, and I thank the Lord for it every day. God, to me, is my very first angel that day, and I've had other angels in my life as well.

I didn't recognize it at the time, but looking back, I see that my first husband's mother was an angel. She taught me everything I needed to know. She showed me how to be a mother, a wife, and a daughter. She taught me how to cook and clean, how to listen, and how to be a true friend.

As she grew older and began to experience Alzheimer's, I was there for her at every moment. Similarly, when Bruce's mom was diagnosed with Alzheimer's, I was there for her as well. We support each other without even realizing how much we have become like angels for one another. My grandmother was truly an angel in my life.

When Dad gained custody of us, he would go visit my grandmother, taking us kids to spend holidays with her. She would then tell our birth mom where we were living. That's how our mom kept track of us. Dad never found out. He had died before I found out.

I feel that my editor is an angel giving me the opportunity to share my life's story and testimony. The way we met was truly by the grace of God. I have been trying my best to get started on this book but couldn't find a way. As I said, angels are always around us.

I still remember receiving a phone call about an eBook platform through Google that had a special on publishing a book and asking if I was interested. I would have a manager providing unlimited editing until the book met my exact satisfaction. This book serves as proof that a prayer can be answered.

This is why we need to live our lives the way God wants us to, so we become examples for the non-believers. This makes us angels to them.

Chapter 5: When Dreams Shatter

At times, dreams are the only thing that keeps you going. For me, a dream is a vivid tapestry of images, emotions, and thoughts, often merged into a convincing story by the subconscious mind while you're asleep. I, too, had a dream— one that I believe dwells in every girl's heart. But that was more than just a dream; it was an enthralling vision fueled by hope and desire. Back then, I believed in making sure that every dream of mine became real.

Beyond the Brink: The Woman Who Refused to Quit

I grew up believing that if I worked hard and followed my plans, I could achieve my dream. I always dreamt of meeting *the one*, the same old cliché: falling in love, getting married, having children, and building a happy life together. I imagined growing old with my husband, surrounded by grandchildren and great-grandchildren, celebrating holidays with big gatherings full of love and laughter. That was my idea of a *perfect life*.

This is where life comes at you unexpectedly. Many things didn't turn out the way I had dreamed. Over time, my dreams began to crumble and eventually turned into one of those black-and-white movies. You can only watch it and reminisce about it all the time. Even as a child, my sister and I escaped into our own realms of imagination. Those realms were more than enough to comfort us at that time. Instead of playing with dolls and dream houses like normal kids, we pretended to explore forests, clean imaginary cabins, or act out weddings with towels draped over our heads as veils.

It took a long time, but it didn't take that long for my dreams and me to shatter because my dreams weren't just dreams. They were *nightmares*. And for the most part, my dreams seemed to get shattered regularly.

We didn't realize it then, but those playful dreams were ways to escape a reality we couldn't quite grasp. As I got older,

I did what I thought I needed to do to attract attention and find love. I was barely a teenager when I started dressing up and wearing makeup that wasn't appropriate for my age, hoping it would bring me closer to the life I dreamed of. Hoping to get the love and attention I was always deprived of. But those hopes didn't lead to happiness. My early relationships were complicated and left a traumatic void that I'll never get rid of.

In my teenage years, I was made to have sex twice because I let my sister-in-law take me to one of those NCO clubs to dance with the men there. I lied my way into that club with the fake IDs we had. My sister-in-law put one of her driver's licenses into my fake ID, which worked out very well in our favor. My looks always made me seem old enough, and I looked a lot like my sister-in-law, so I was never carded. She got carded, though; *I didn't. I looked old enough, so I always lied to these men.*

I met many men that day. One man stayed unconformably close to me that night throughout the dance. He kept me company all night, never letting me out of sight. How we met is another story. Things got worse, as he wanted to have fun in the club. He took me to an excluded park where he forced sex on me. This led to me getting separated from my sister-in-law. I had to call my dad to pick me up that night.

At the very end, I had to be put on a bus to get home. But he wouldn't put me on that bus unless I had sex again. I was treated inappropriately twice because I was left alone, and he wouldn't take no for an answer. It didn't matter if I wanted it or not; *I was just too afraid to say no.* I later learned this was called date rape.

That was the moment I truly felt spoiled in my mind. I was unaware of the full extent of the consequences since I was still in high school. Every guy I dated considered me spoiled. I gave in to every boy I dated and was seen as the girl who gave in to every boy she was with. I had that reputation. My reputation was quite ironic. I was that girl who spread her legs for every man I was with. I was afraid to say no because I thought I wouldn't be liked. The reality was brutal.

I only dated three men throughout my high school years. I dated the first guy I went out with because he promised to marry me, and then he attempted to murder me when I tried to break up with him. The second one defended me whenever he found out that I had been wronged, but unfortunately, his life was short-lived as he was killed tragically in a motorcycle accident.

I genuinely wanted to settle down with the last guy, so I decided to come clean and tell him the truth. I was going to try and get my life together, so I told him I wouldn't do anything until after we got out of school.

Eventually, back in high school, I met someone who seemed to offer a fresh start. He proposed to me over Christmas vacation, and we finally married during my senior year of high school. For a while, I thought I was finally building the life I had always wanted.

I got into the same loophole all over again when a football team coach approached me, as he knew I was in an art class. He told me he wanted me to come to his room to paint a mascot on the football that he would give at the football banquet, which was a big thing back then. He got permission for me to leave the study hall to come and paint the football in his office, which is above the auditorium and next to the dressing room by the basketball courts. The very first time I went there, he approached me. My dreams were shattered again.

What happened that day is something I still can't process. He tried to touch my breast, and he asked me how it felt to be married and have sex all the time. I never told Jim, my husband, because he would've beaten the coach to a pulp. I never told anybody because I didn't want to get anyone in trouble. I feared the consequences of it all.

To this day, I remember that Jim's dad always told the story of first meeting me. When I met him, I walked by the kitchen table, and his dad commented on how short my skirt was and how the hem of my skirt touched the top of the table when I walked by.

Right after that, I quit wearing makeup and short skirts. I mostly wore jeans. So, I was back to fooling myself into thinking I was anything but spoiled goods.

But even then, the cracks began to show. My ex-husband, Jim, asked me for a divorce just months before our 25th wedding anniversary. I later learned he had been unfaithful to me for 16 years of our 25 year marriage. The realization left me *shattered*. Despite everything I had tried to be a loving wife, a stay-at-home mom, and someone who gave her all. I felt like I had failed. It was not a one-time thing, Jim cheated several times.

When I returned to work after years of being at home, I faced new trials. I tried my hardest to learn how to cook, clean, and be the person everyone thought I was.

My struggles with perfectionism were always disregarded as unserious. People would complain that this habit of mine was nothing but hoarding. I was termed too crazy and too perfect, to the point that I was diagnosed with OCD. It was the culprit all along that made even simple tasks overwhelming.

I would drag everything out to clean, but in the end, I never managed to finish. I felt stuck in a cycle of chaos, exhaustion, and self-doubt.

I somehow wished to find some support from my children. They had their own ways of coming to terms with life; as my children grew older, they began to find their own paths. Things started hitting me hard when my daughters were in high school and college while my son had dropped out. I was losing the marriage I thought was going strong, along with the sense of purpose I had built around it. My life felt like it was slipping through my fingers, and I was left to pick up the pieces.

I was tired, lost, and isolated. The dreams I once held so tightly seemed like distant memories, replaced by a reality I never could have imagined. Yet, through it all, I've held on, trying to rediscover who I am and what I want from the life I still have ahead of me.

Chapter 6: Extending the Arithmetic of Life to Choosing to Live Not Just Survive

For many years, I have always asked myself one burning question: *Why am I so unhappy? Why am I never satisfied? Why don't things ever work in my favor?* Drama and hardship seemed to lace themselves into the fabric of my life, and with every passing day, I felt the weight of sadness growing heavier. Depression wasn't just an occasional visitor; it had made itself at home. I was the loving, welcoming host, and it was a parasite waiting to feed on my helplessness.

Beyond the Brink: The Woman Who Refused to Quit

I fooled myself for a long time, telling myself that life's ups and downs were part of maturing and that I could power through and feel stronger. But deep down, I didn't understand what it meant to be truly happy or how to get there. I watched others go about their lives, laughing and glowing with a kind of inner joy that felt utterly foreign to me. I always felt left out; I didn't deserve to experience good things in life. One could say I even started projecting these things to people around me.

It was a bullet trigger point for that one day, I decided to search for answers. I knew I needed to dig deep, ask hard questions, and confront the truth about myself and my life.

I began by recognizing that life doesn't stop people from moving forward. We are shaped by the events we experience, the people we love, and the losses we endure. To understand my long cycles of melancholy, I had to look back and unravel every moment of my life, starting with my childhood—where my world was first turned upside down when our father gained custody of us in third grade. That wasn't traumatic for me but later, in 1973, when I got married. That was the long period of my life when I was truly unhappy and at my lowest.

That year, I got married, and the first snaps in my understanding of happiness came with it. The 51 years that followed 1973 to 2024 became an epic of weddings, funerals, and countless upheavals. I deeply fear change; no matter how hard I try, I cannot overcome the fact that things will change eventually, whether for the better or the absolute worse.

The same change can bring both death and joy. Despite all the peaks and joys that should have brought happiness, I remained trapped in a cycle of unhappiness.

I had two marriages, and neither brought me the anticipation I hoped for. I saw two of my siblings getting married and then celebrating the weddings of my three children. Yet even these cheerful moments carried their weight of stress. On top of that, life sent devastating challenges to my way: *my oldest daughter lost one house to a fire and another to a tornado.* She came to live with me both times, and I helped her rebuild. Each step had a brief period at times when we had to learn to adapt and continue.

But the darkest shadows were cast by loss. Over those five decades, I attended more funerals than I can count. I lost two husbands, both sets of their parents, my own mother, father, stepmother, and stepfather. I lost two siblings, several grandparents, aunts, uncles, and countless extended family members.

Grief grew on me; it was a part of my life by then. I barely had time to heal from one loss before another came crashing into my life. The grief never ended, it just layered deeper into my soul. But in my case, I had so many different people pass away that the greetings process never ended.

Depression isn't just emotional; *it manifests physically, too.* Many don't talk about it, but depression slowly eats you. For years, I experienced aches with unexplained symptoms and a deep, pervasive fatigue. At one point, I was even misdiagnosed with narcolepsy because I would blackout unexpectedly, even mid-conversation. I once drove 30 miles without any memory of the journey. It ended in a car wreck; *one I have no recollection of.* It's already been five years since the near fatal one car accident.

Later, a therapist would tell me this wasn't narcolepsy at all but a form of post-traumatic stress. It all made sense there and then. My body and mind had been carrying the weight of decades of trauma, and they were shutting down as a means of survival. The feeling of seeing your body betraying you isn't a good one.

I can be talking to you just as I'm talking to you now, and I will fall asleep and not even know that I've fallen asleep. I was at a counselor's, talking to my therapist, and I thought I was still talking to her when, all of a sudden, I woke up and came out of it. She told me I had continued to talk the whole time I was sleeping. She said that this was a form of post-traumatic stress. Even though I had been diagnosed with narcolepsy, she changed it to post-traumatic stress because it wasn't.

But I've realized that survival alone isn't enough anymore. That car wreck was a wake-up call. It forced me to see that I've spent my life just existing, moving from one day to the next, from one challenge to the next without truly living.

I need to see life in a different way. I want to be thankful and build trust in myself. I want to acknowledge my struggles and start loving myself more. I want to gain confidence more than ever. Life can never be a straight path; it's a never-ending spiral.

That's exactly why I'm writing this book. I'm tired of simply existing. I want to live. I want to find joy, experience what's left of my dreams, and embrace a love for the future. I want to teach others what I've learned and help them find their own paths to happiness. Life has been hard, but I refuse to let the hardships define me. This is my choice to live, not just to survive and I hope my journey inspires others to do the same.

I could tell many more stories of abuse and unfair treatment but I am trying my best to put the past away and not let it control my life.

Chapter 7: Skeletons In the Closet

The only way I can do justice to my experiences is to talk more about them. That's where the phrase *"skeletons in the closet"* feels the perfect way to describe what I have lived through all these past years. On the surface, everything looks *picture-perfect*. I got married and had many kids, a home, and a life, but I carry this haunting truth beneath it all. I felt so alone, even when we sat in the same room. It felt like I was invisible, and my feelings didn't matter. I experienced similar feelings outside of my marriage.

40

You can't blame everyone around you all the time. Sometimes, you need to take a stand for yourself, and that's what I did. I tried to open up many times to talk about how I felt, but it was like my words would hit an empty wall and fall to the floor always discarded behind as unheard and unrecognized. It's so painful to realize that I'm always in a position where I was never taken seriously, where my demands and emotions were dismissed as if they were nothing. I never felt at home. The absence, I feel, isn't just always physical, it's emotional too.

There's always this looming shadow, the constant feeling that something between us isn't being said. I can't shake the suspicion or the weight of wondering if I'm sharing my life with someone whose heart is elsewhere. It's like I'm living with a ghost, someone here in body but not in mind or spirit.

I felt like I was carrying the burden of that marriage all on my own, and it was exhausting. I had started to doubt myself, *was I not enough? Was I unworthy of love? How did I end up in a situation where I felt so small and unseen?* It was like this secret, this skeleton in the closet, that had defined our relationship then, even if it had never been spoken out loud. *And that silence?* That had been the loudest part of all.

I've always had my fair share of stories I haven't told anybody. I've always been afraid to share them. Some of these stories are beyond hurtful; to some extent, they are so vile that whenever I think about them, I get a stabbing pain in my forehead and blurriness, and I almost feel like I'm going to black out. And then I just feel guilty all over again.

Trauma only makes you normalize all the bad things around you. The only way I can do justice to my experience is by confronting these stories and saying them out loud. If these stories negatively affect you, you also face a challenge that needs confronting. I'm not alone in experiencing this, which is why I am sharing these stories and bringing them to the light.

My earliest memories are of my childhood. When I was living in Kansas back in the sixth grade, I was woken up by my older stepbrother and was told that I needed to go downstairs. I never developed a strong relationship with my stepsiblings, which made me always keep my guard up in their presence. My stepbrother and I clashed a lot, and I found it difficult to trust him.

I still went with him. Now that I think of it, it was because he was so much like my stepmother that I started disliking him to no end. He trailed behind my siblings and me as we made our way to the living room, where we were instructed to form a line. My stepmother informed us that my stepbrother had discovered me smoking in my closet. We were instructed to line up to verify this claim and given a cigarette to try.

I wasn't surprised; I anticipated this. When they counted to three, we were told to take a puff. Back in sixth grade, I thought, *"What use do I have for a simple cigarette?"* I had no intention of participating. I wanted to prove a point to my stepmother. There was no way I was going to inhale; I had never smoked before.

I had no reason to force that nasty stuff into my lungs. The chain of events was pretty simple. My two younger siblings started coughing and choking. Then, my stepbrother, who was older than me, began to cough and choke. After that, all eyes were on *me*.

I never got to do anything because I refused to breathe in. I did not inhale. This decision did not turn out well for me; it backfired immediately. I faced harsh punishment without any justification.

I never experienced any negative effects from smoking because I didn't allow it. That wasn't the part of the story that had such an adverse effect on me. The punishment that came from that day hurt and caused the most damage. They were nothing but embarrassing, degrading, and belittling. I was in the 6th grade, old enough to think I knew everything, but I was made to lie down on the bed while tea towels were pinned to my bottom as if I were wearing a diaper.

I was then given a baby pacifier and told to put it in my mouth. I was forced to go outside in the small community of about 600 people and walk along the sidewalk around the perimeter of the small community. That was so hurtful to me because I knew that all my classmates lived in those blocks that I was to walk, and they would see me in that diaper, with that pacifier in my mouth.

The following day, I went to school and faced the teasing and torment that would haunt me for years. It took a long time to recover. It still hurts. The only thing that helped was our move to Arkansas soon after, which allowed me to escape it. I never mentioned it again until now, as I reflect on it.

Now, at the age of 69, that one puff of a cigarette was the only cigarette I had ever smoked in my life until marijuana came to my awareness. And I haven't smoked it.

I breathe in the smoke because it helps with the aches and pains. But I don't even smoke it because of my hatred for smoking. I've lived with that hurt all my life. Then, there was another degrading story that happened in the seventh grade. It's a story that, until you read it in this book, you will have never heard me say what it was.

My job was to clean the house after school, babysit my nephew, cook supper, help with homework, do my own homework, and clean up afterwards. By then, my stepmom would come home from work. If there was anything else she wanted me to do, I had to do it no matter what. She had several pets that I also had to pick up after. These pets were like her babies, and it was my job to clean up the feces on the floor. That day, I forgot and left it under the coffee table. A simple mistake that caused me so much pain.

I had forgotten all about it. I had too much on my plate; she found it when she returned from school. I was told to pick it up with my hands and put it in my mouth. I refused, and that was the wrong thing to do. What she did next was something I never saw coming. She grabbed it, crammed it into my mouth and forced me to take a bite.

The tears were in my eyes, and I pushed them away, trying to escape her. She slapped me, and I would always fight back. That only meant one thing at the end of the day. I would receive a spanking with the belt from my dad when he would come home because she would tell on me that I had fought her when she had asked me to do something. She never told him why I fought back because she didn't want to be blamed for causing me to do it. But I got spanked twice that day, on top of having to take a bite of that disgusting thing.

To this day, it hurts to even think about it, but it wasn't the only time my dad took my stepmother's side. I hated getting in trouble just because they would side together. Then, there was a bowl of vinegar in the refrigerator. I was confronted about pouring out that bowl of vinegar from a cucumber salad, the salad where you have cucumbers, onions, and tomatoes soaked in vinegar.

Well, she would use the vinegar to make another salad, and I supposedly didn't know it. And I supposedly poured the vinegar out, and she was going to spank me for pouring it out. I didn't know who dumped the vinegar out, but it wasn't me. And I wasn't going to be punished for doing it. Well, I got tied to the bed and was beaten, and I was told to stay in my room until my dad got home.

When my dad arrived home, he punished me as well, and I was spanked for defending myself. I explained that I was unaware of what happened, but she called me a liar, which prompted my reaction. After I received the second spanking, my father confessed that he was the one who had poured out the vinegar. In total, I received two spankings from him.

They say betrayal comes from your enemies, but mine came from my very own blood. It hurt that they sided together, and then I was still the one who got punished. I couldn't impress either of them. I couldn't go to my friends' houses. I couldn't believe in anything.

There were so many things. I hated being blamed for smoking. I hated being taught to dress like her. I even found jewelry in my chest of drawers because she hid it, and then I'd get in trouble. In short, I hated being compared to her.

It only got worse from there, to the point where I didn't even go to friends' houses because I was blamed when I got home. It was constant, one thing after another. The persistent reminder of how I had been belittled all my life ignited something different in me. I didn't let it all get to me; instead, I decided I needed to get away from that narrative of how it was easy to use and discard me right after. I needed to rid myself of my skeletons first to get somewhere in life. *It was now or never.*

Chapter 8: Reinventing Purpose

Battling through all these circumstances, my life has been marked by numerous ups and downs, filled with lots of drama and tragedy. I have taken a look back in time to reflect on some of the different scenarios that have caused me hurt and confusion. During many therapy sessions, I realized that I had experienced a variety of forms of abuse throughout my life.

The dictionary defines *"abuse"* as use of a harmful effect or misuse, to treat with cruelty and violence, to use in a way to cause harm. There are three elements of the word abuse, and they are abuse, abused, and a crisis. There are other types of abuse which include: *Physical, Mental, Verbal, Psychological, Emotional, Neglect, Domestic, Sexual, Financial, Modern Slavery*, and last but not the least *self-neglect*.

As a scout leader, I received training on abuse prevention, including sexual abuse. This training has allowed me to look back at my life, and it helped me to become aware of just how abused I was in the past as a youth.

This training has also made me understand the lasting impact it had on my teenage and early adult years. I always tried to teach my friends and children how to become better persons, but I wasn't always successful, because I still had my own problems and challenges that I tried to keep hidden.

After a major car accident in *January 2020*, I found myself laid up in a hospital bed for seven months with lots of time to think about the past. I knew that I was lucky to be alive, but I wondered *"Why I was given a second chance at life?"*

All of the evidence indicated that I should have died in the car wreck, but surprisingly, I'm still alive. Several times, I started trying to write about the miracles of how I survived the wreck, but it wasn't until I was approached to actually write a book, that I truly began to explore my story.

It was when I was asked to write an autobiography that I began to really think about it. I put all my notes together and started to learn to lean towards writing the autobiography rather than the story of my car wreck, which I had thought about writing.

In my opinion, if I could offer hope to others, showing that change is possible from all of the different abuses, I would have helped others free of any abuse. This means that I could look back at my past, figure out what I could change, and then how to change it.

I realized that education is the first step to change, and I have done the best I can to learn all I can. Now, I am at the point where I am actively working to change what I can.

At heart, I am a teacher. It is in my nature to tell the world that I'm not perfect and that's fine. I have been abused, and I don't want to abuse others in any way. Once I share my story, I hope to create new, happy stories that don't include abuse. As I write this book, I recognize how many painful memories I carry and relive them each time I share my experiences.

Yet I am learning to be more forgiving, to do things differently, and to make more mature decisions. I can now realize that I'm forgiving myself of things that I couldn't before.

I now have an attitude of *letting it go*, and I'm finding new priorities in life. That's how I am reinventing a new life. My priorities and my future will have a better purpose because of it. I have a new priority that I say helps me in my cause.

I have a new prayer that I say each day. It goes:

"Dear God, help me reinvent myself and guide me to go back to where I need to be. I need to be a disciple that you intend me to be. Open my eyes, and allow me lead others towards your loving arms. Let me be joyful in my journey. Let my path be smooth as we walk your path. If I am to walk alone without my loved ones, let me love the ones I walk with. Let me always know what is important and help me to forgive what is not in forget what is not important."

This prayer has given me a new purpose in life. It helps me see things in a different light. It helps put past in the past.

Chapter 9: The Woman Who Refused to Quit

As I move forward praying for my future, some have called me stubborn, others have called me hard-headed, but I call myself a *survivor*. Above all, I know that God calls me *"His"*. God has always had a path for me to walk. He's always given a path with purpose but sometimes that path has been rockier than others at times. The car wreck that I survived through was so near-death experience, one where I should not have lived.

Now, I realize that I am alive because God has a purpose for me. He has another path for me to walk. Whether here on earth or in heaven, even though there are many realms of my life, I'm in need of Him in my life and He needs my work. I am aware that I am still a work in progress, and my sense of purpose is shifting. At this point, I have come to realize that my purposes are changing, and I have no idea where I will be or what I will become.

I have just learned that I am going to take a different path in life that I wasn't prepared for. For Thirty-years, I have trained for a job that gave me great reward; *Boy scouting.*

I love teaching and sharing what I have learned with others. I take great pride in calling myself a survivor and in knowing that I have a purpose for being a scout, *a Boy Scout adult*. It was this purpose that helped me not quit.

It was the purpose that kept me going. One thing I have learned is always to be prepared, not to be surprised and caught off guard so that we can claim a new purpose from what my car wreck could show me. *My car wreck showed me that I am a miracle.*

Nevertheless, I mostly lay in wonder at what was to be. I lay broken, unable to move, wondering, *"Why should I even try? What I wanted to do was move forward."* I was going to have to start all over; I would not be doing scouts anymore.

I just have to learn new skills and will need to find another purpose to keep me going this time. Then I got a strange phone call about writing this book, and that gave me hope not to quit.

I could use my writing skills as healing, questioning where I was heading, and the answer was in writing this book. As I write the book, it was hard to go through because I had to do the research. However, I had taken several journalism classes in high school and college. I had a little bit of training as I began to write, but still I needed a subject.

I simply wanted something more than just a car wreck to write about. I decided to write an autobiography. I had several piles of notes from the past, but they never felt quite right. I have compiled all of my notes together, placed them in a folder, and given up the possibility of a book.

The opportunity came unexpectedly through eBooks, and Google called about writing this book. They gave me a deal that I could not pass up, and it has been the best decision that I've ever made.

I talked to my therapist, whom I talk to once a week, and he advised me that it would be therapeutic. I shared my past stories and worked through them to write about them.

Now, I have been able to feel peace inside, peace that I haven't felt in a long time. It's been a challenge, but I'm making progress. I now feel stronger and more capable of overcoming challenges I never thought possible.

I am incredibly thankful for opening this doorway and helping me put my past behind me, learn from my mistakes, and reach out to do the Lord's work. It makes me feel so *lucky* and *fortunate*.

Recently, I was informed that my daughters planned to gather to celebrate Christmas on Friday, the 13th. They came to me and told me that they would come pick me up, and we would celebrate this holiday on Friday, the 13th.

I initially insisted when they invited me to join them. Friday the 13th has always been associated with bad luck, and I felt that it was an inappropriate day to celebrate *Christ's birth*.

I told my girls not to come get me. I stood up to them for the first time. I did not go to Christmas for my family even though I knew I would miss seeing my grandkids and seeing everybody. But it made me feel good that I stood up not to celebrate the Lord's birthday on such a bad luck day.

If we couldn't do it on Christmas, then it wasn't worth doing. I ended up spending Christmas and New Year's Day by myself. My friend who usually came was not able to come because the girls couldn't bring him, but I felt at peace at heart that I had made the right decision. My heart was at peace.

Beyond the Brink: The Woman Who Refused to Quit

Before I embarked on this writing journey, I would have gone with my girls out of fear of missing out on something. And for the first time, I had peace that I could do things on my own even though I was stuck in a wheelchair, and I was not walking yet.

Life has presented me with so many things. It's given me a new purpose to live again, and even with this, it's given me a chance to see myself in a different light.

I've learned that I can do things on my own. I now have somebody different who brings me groceries, and their family has helped do things for me and helped make some repairs.

I've started reaching out to others for help rather than my own kids. It has made me a stronger person, and it helps me feel strong inside. I feel that I can face just about anything now.

Chapter 10: Beyond The Brink

There always comes a time in life when we need to stand firm in our beliefs, even when the world around us shifts like sand beneath our feet. If I talk about myself, I have lived through countless experiences of sorrow, joy, loss, and love, and I have come to understand that our journey is not without reason.

No one in this world is born without a purpose. We were all created for a reason, and none of our actions and struggles will ever go to waste.

Beyond the Brink: The Woman Who Refused to Quit

My days have been filled with many eye-opening lessons. Some were learned the hard way, but all have led me closer to the truth my Father in heaven has set before me. I am blessed with children, grandchildren, and great-grandchildren who happily seek my guidance, and I strive to show them the way.

My path has never been easy; *my heart is filled with many regrets.* These same regrets have taken me where I am *today.* The time has come to stand up for what is right, to listen to God's voice, and to prepare for the calling that will one day lead us all home.

Now, when I talk about going beyond the brink, it means to go where something drastic is about to happen. I am now 69 years old. I have survived two husbands who have been laid to rest. My great-grandchildren call me *Doctor NoNo* because I have treated their little boo-boos and taught them the meaning of *No.* I correct them when they misbehave but love them when they are good.

I teach them the difference between right and wrong, but my own children have not always listened to me. I have many regrets in life. I regret that I could not always be strong for them, but I have now reached a point where I must stand up for myself regarding *right and wrong* for the Lord, my Savior, and our Almighty Father.

I have been nothing but privileged to guide those around me. My Father wants me to teach others what it means to follow and believe the teachings of our Lord. Our knowledge is the core. So now, if the time is coming, we should look at the skies for the signs of the Father. The signs are *everywhere*. They're within us.

To stay true to our path, we must read the Bible, reflect on His words, examine our hearts, look deep within our souls, and listen thoughtfully to discern what God instructs us to do in order to follow the path chosen for each of us. I read the word but don't always grasp it fully or ask enough questions when I do. I need to keep learning my lessons repeatedly.

I don't consider myself a saint. I have made many mistakes, even while pleasing my Father. When I realized I was making the same mistakes repeatedly and was no closer to my goals, I deepened my prayers, asking to be shown what I was doing wrong. I took my time to listen for guidance on the right path. I began to find a sense of peace within myself and started to see visions of what was needed.

My visions come to me in dreams while I sleep. I always wake up knowing what I need to do, and a peaceful sensation will wash over me, providing comfort and a sense of strength as I fulfill what is expected of me.

I just knew that what I did was right. I did not feel overly proud or cocky. I just knew that it was the right thing to do. Not everyone was behind me. *Did everyone agree with me or with my actions?* I felt at peace every time because I believed I was making the right choice.

As for others, I cannot make the choices for you, and you cannot make the choices for me. We will know what we have been taught, and we must listen with an understanding of what the Father asks of us.

I believe that each kingdom has its own god or leader and each of those kingdoms have different beliefs on religion. But there is one God over all of the others that stands above the rest. An example is the belief in the Roman gods; *the Catholics, the Protestants, and the Baptists all have their leaders.* But God is above them all.

People look up to leaders, but leaders must look to the one true heavenly Father. Then, we'll know that our leader is right. We are always taught to look at each leader as a leader of kingdoms at religion simply as leaders have to look to this father on high. In this country, the one leader is the president.

Do not mistake this man for a god but as a leader. A Prayer: *Pray that this leader moves to the path of the true God. It is important that these leaders never consider themselves gods but are the leaders God wants them to be. We are each given a choice, hence, to vote for the president and to let him pray for guidance, and it is up to us to put the man in the right position. That is the same with God.*

We look at a leader who must be what God wants. A leader must be god-fearing. And if we find a leader who doesn't live by God, then it falls upon the voters who voted him in. Also, remember not to go with the majority, where we will be judged separately, so our leaders cannot judge us except for God.

Each person must choose who he follows, and God will judge them according to what he asks of them. I pray a little prayer each day, and that prayer is all due to God. God, for me, is the Father of all leaders and my Father on high. Grant me peace as I walk the path laid out for my journey.

Let the path be smooth without rocks or crevices. Let me remember for my enemies maybe few, and let my followers be many as we walk the path leading to our kingdom.

Let us each walk as disciples, making us teachers of men, teachers of your word, and examples of your life. Let each of us be an example that we would want others to see through our eyes, upon us an example, passing this down to others under us by being an example. Then, we can teach using our words, actions, and examples. All of us are one. We don't get to choose the Lord; *the Lord chooses you.*

My Father guides me, and I will now guide others in my choices and give you peace in the coming days. Let your choice of Lord be made and follow him down the path and his faith in you. I use this as an example of my life, and this is what I do. I hope to put the past behind me and use this example to lead others. That is how I stay strong and keep going. I know that I'm walking the right path.

Having faith and following a straight path is one of the hardest things a person can do. Life will never be a smooth road but filled with many detours, broken roads, and moments of doubt that test even the strongest believers. Staying true and faithful is not just about belief. It is about endurance, discipline, and the willingness to keep going even when everything around you feels uncertain. Even when you're at your lowest, you must keep on living.

One of the biggest struggles is that faith often requires trusting in what we cannot see. We do not see God but know He is always around us. When life is painful, prayers seem unanswered, or the world feels chaotic, it is easy to question whether God is truly guiding us or whether he is actually there. We may start strong, but our faith can feel fragile when hardship comes, whether through loss, betrayal, sickness, or loneliness. There is always a greater temptation to take an easier path.

Another challenge is that the world does not always support faith. Society values power, success, and self-reliance, while faith calls us to humility, patience, and dependence on God. Walking a straight path means resisting all sorts of distractions and temptations that distract us from the final truth. It means choosing righteousness when others around us take shortcuts. It means believing in God's plan when we cannot yet see the destination.

Even in the Bible, we see how hard it is to remain faithful. *Peter* walked on water but sank when fear overtook him. *Moses* doubted himself even when God spoke to him directly. *David*, a man after God's own heart, fell into temptation. If these great figures struggled, it is no surprise that we do too.

But faith is not always about perfection. It is about persistence, over and over again. The path is never meant to be easy, but it is worth walking. Every time we choose to trust God despite any uncertainty, we grow stronger. Every time we pray, instead of giving up, we build our faith, no matter how fragile it is. Walking with God is a daily choice, and though we may stumble, He is always there to help us back up.

We do not walk this path alone or choose it blindly. God has given us the wisdom to seek His truth, hear His voice, and follow His direction. The world is filled with many leaders, but there is only one true King, and it is to Him we must turn our eyes. The time is near when we will be called, and we must be ready.

Our decisions shape our journey, and our faith will lead the way. I have made my choice and will walk this path with nothing but utter strength and conviction. My heart is set on the Father, and my hope is in His promise. Let us now go forward in faith, knowing that all our steps are guided, our hearts are watched over, and our souls are held in the hands of the Almighty, *for he can foresee things we can't.*

www.ingramcontent.com/pod-product-compliance
Lightning Source LLC
Chambersburg PA
CBHW051331120626
46547CB00016B/2499